Lost Thinker
Unchained Melodies of Melancholy Harmonies

Collected Poems

by
Ross Leishman

Lost Thinker

Unchained Melodies of Melancholy Harmonies

Collected Poems

by
Ross Leishman

Lost Thinker:
Unchained Melodies of Melancholy Harmonies

By Ross Leishman

First Edition

Author: Ross Leishman
Editor: Paul Gilliland
Formatting: Southern Arizona Press
Cover Artwork: Ross Leishman

Published by Southern Arizona Press
Sierra Vista, Arizona 85635
www.SouthernArizonaPress.com

ISBN: 978-1-960038-23-4

Poetry

Acknowledgements

To my wife Shelley, for her untiring support,
help with the technical bits, patience, and love.

And to my three children: Darceah, Bryn, and Bonnie,
for their love and encouragement.

Contents

Freshly trimmed, combed, and slicked back in the bathroom mirror of my mind …

Delicate Things

Softy floating,
petal like in their existence,
gently tumbling,
head over heels,
without the earth's resistance,
subtle flames flickering,
like a time worn guitarists gentle finger picking.

Delicate Things, like when Jeff Buckley sings,
and like him, gone too soon,
when the girls swoon,
springs first daffodils bloom.

The colours of our lives,
those gorgeous, enchanted butterflies,
so brief is their time,
how delicate and how fine,
butterflies,
tiny, winged souls of the recently departed,
keeping watch over the loved ones of their lives,
the left behind and the broken hearted.

*Freshly hoovered, steam mopped and polished in the
dining room of my mind …*

My Soundproof Soul

Hush.
Can you hear the pain aching in my soul,
silent but obsequious,
her name only heard in whispers and moans,
drifting on the wings of crack infused dragonflies,
strung out for miles,
lost in the summer haze,
crash landing in a daze,
their powerful wings beating so silently,
like the fluid mechanics of my robotic soul,
going through the motions,
savouring the emotions
till suddenly they're still.

Silence,
nothing moves,
nothing is said,
it's just the empty silence.

in my soul.

*Freshly recorded on to a C90 cassette and played loud ,
the 80s mix tape of my life played on the pioneer stereo
system of my mind ...*

My Heroes

Fade into me,
fade into you,
out of the depths of my depression,
on the wings of my obsession,
life imitates art,
the soundtrack of my soul,
performed by godlike musicians
that unfortunately still suffer from that terminal human
frailty.

Images of me,
images of you,
a life once lived,
in some cracked rear- view,
that Rockstar death wish that no one ever knew,
where have all the flowers gone,
where are the writers of all those sad songs,
I wish they could all live.

EVERLONG.

*Freshly planted, tendered to, and watered in the
allotment of my mind ...*

Lover Within

Come and take my hand and lead me from this place of
sorrow,
cold and dead inside,
with nowhere on this earth to hide,
a brush of your lips or a shoulder just to cling to,
my mind plays tricks,
while wild thoughts smolder just below the surface.

I saw you across the crowded room,
but all you saw was a walking voice behind a smiling
mask, aching under a heartless moon.

My life jumps from one fantasy to the next,
one paperback novel to another,
an empty room lit by a naked bulb,
the only company I get to keep is my Lover Within,
but never deeper than my own shed skin.

*Freshly collected from life's leftovers discarded in haste
on the lonely quicksand beach of my mind ...*

Lana del Rey Eyes

Autumn, winter, spring,
summertime sadness,
that look, that voice,
those Lana del Rey eyes,
just make you wanna cry.

The voice of a fallen angel,
the gorgeous storyteller
stuck between gods and monsters
reading bedtime stories to naughty boys.

The accidental actress,
so good at playing her part, life.

Life imitates art.

Forbidden fruit that tastes like Pepsi cola,
lost in her watercolour skies,
just, just because.

Oh, those Lana del Rey Eyes.

*Freshly picked, wilted down and served with some garlic
mash and lamb shanks in the gourmet kitchen
of my mind …*

Importance

To know one's place in society,
to feel like you're not in a minority,
to have to answer to a higher authority,
Importance.

To really know that you are loved,
to really have faith in something above,
to know that one mellopuff is never enough,
Importance.

The importance of feeling important,
the necessity of our own complexity,
the reality of our unbalanced Morality,
Importance.

Searching for our role in the universe,
knowing you never made anyone's life worse,
You are a blessing, never a Curse,
The importance of feeling important.
You are important.

*Freshly removed from its packet, spread with margarine,
and sprinkled with 100s and 1000s in the kindergarten
lunchroom of my mind …*

How to Look Good Dead

Inspired by real life,
"life imitates art",
go with grace,
a pretty face
but a mind as dirty
as an industrial skyline.

Intelligently, breathtakingly,
cool to the touch,
unmistakably and unshakably,
oh, I need you so much.

Day dreamer, true believer,
thought stealer,
black market imagination dealer.

The truth, immune to it,
the honesty of our dishonesty,
the insanity of our incoming calamity,
the loss of sanctity.

Dream, dream delicately, dream deeply,

Obsequiously and deviously,
sour to the taste,
a bittersweet pill to swallow,
a freshly dug forever home, but
but not too shallow.

Freshly put in a bowl, heated for 60 seconds, and drizzled over homemade Reese's cups in the country kitchen of my mind ...

Heavy

Drowning in "what ifs" and procrastination,

My knees buckle under the weight of anticipation.

Heavy, on my mind,
tightness around my heart,
so much easier to follow than it is to lead,
easier to break sometimes than it is to bleed,
change is a coming,

Do I throw my hat in the ring?
Do I look for a way out,
or I finally let my inner voice sing.

Choices, my therapist says "don't listen to the voices,"
but when we have to choose,
there's the weight of "but what if, I lose."

Sad but true.

Freshly unzipped, slid down, and hung on the jeweled
jumpsuit hanger of my mind ...

An American Tragedy

Oh, I wish I was …
such poignant words,
the power and the beauty of such
a God given voice,
my ears have ever heard ...

That human condition,
the greed inside,
Colonel of the fairground ride,
criminal snowman,
corrupter of the ultimate showman.

An American trilogy,
one of my all-time favourite inspirational songs,
Elvis Aaron Presley,
an American Tragedy,
crossing the colour, race, and religion
Grand Canyon of narcissism,
undone by a man's talent for deception
wrapped up in a star-spangled banner
or fried peanut butter sandwich menu selection,
but still plain ole goddam human GREED.

They say build it and they will come,
sing it out loud and they will listen,
teach and they will learn ...
But will we ever … learn?
Look away, look away Dixieland.

*Freshly planted, watered, and tendered then picked and
arranged in the Murano vase of my mind ...*

Flowers of My Soul

Delicately crafted,
intricately folded,
a flowery thing to behold.

All the colours of the rainbow,
that match the forever changing moods of my suffering
soul.

Paper thin,
the shape within,
the shape of my heart,
engineered in origami art.

Standing tall but not of the tall poppy kind,

Staunch and not stifled,
gorgeous and recycled,
no limited shelf life here,
I can see their beauty for years and years.

unless I set fire to them.

*Freshly sanded, smoothed, and varnished, in the moody
little man shed of my mind …*

Drop in the Ocean

In these times of sickness, war, and sorrow,
it's easy to wonder,
what if there's no tomorrow ...

Pain, grief, shame,
Pain soaked in heartache,
Pain wrapped up in a delicate candy shell,
the sadness in its relief
but as devious as a clockwork thief.

Just a drop in the ocean ...
I heard myself say
but the bigger the river,
the bigger the flood.
The deeper the wound,
the darker the blood.

I get it though ...
life happens,
shit happens,
life and death happens ...

Sometimes it can just seem like such a long and lonely
road,
littered with broken bottles, promises, and good
intentions,
on your way to find your place in the world,
perhaps a little self-redemption ...

A famous blonde once said ...
"It may not happen overnight,   but it will happen."

Freshly turned over, fertilized, and planted out in radishes, carrots, and potatoes in the raised garden of my mind …

Beautiful Morning

In an ideal world,
dogs would yawn with breath like flowers
in the cold, early morning light of day,
it's something a little different.

Beautiful morning,
the cold light of day
has been replaced by the warming, life giving heat
of an early November Southern morning,
gorgeously bright,
soon I'll be wearing my sunglasses at night …
so, I can see. So, I can see.
Beauty abounds, the garden blooms,
fruit trees swelling with anticipation,
mmm, cherries, tomatoes, stone fruit, summer salivation.

If I was an artist, which I'm not,
I would trace from the nape of my love's neck
down her curves to her toes.
I write because I can't paint or draw,
I missed that system upgrade ...
Sometimes I can paint you, with words
like delicate Hershey's kisses dripping off the tongues
of fallen angels drifting in their misplaced faith.

Beautiful morning coffee,
heat haze at 8am,
dogs fight over the sun patch on the carpet
until the French doors are flung open,
release the hounds
I wish our dogs had breath like flowers ...

*Freshly dragged kicking and screaming from the covid
addled dark spaces of my mind …*

Page Turning Heroes

Using my pen like an artist's brush,
delicately dipping into the squeezed-out letters
in the tear stained, soul dripping,
finger dipping pallet of my mind,
letters stick together,
some falling from my pen
never to find their true meaning
on the blurred lines of the page.

Those fortunate letters that made it
are living examples to all the other trillions
in the alphabet nation,
their exploits played out in so many fantastic and creative
ways,
their numerous romances,
   adventures,
      battles,
         and portrayals of everyday,
days of our lives,
life will live on through the eyes
and open minds of anyone willing to read them, oHsere
???? Rearrange them and there you have them.

Heroes

Letters form words
to make our thoughts and dreams
come to life.

Freshly picked off the shelves, and thrown in the grocery trolley of my mind …

Porcelain Frailty

Remember I told you, "You couldn't afford me,"
but you didn't listen,
you just went and adored me,
 too much trouble,
 too much pain,
I took you for granted,
thought our love was in vain.

The eternal cost, the silent Casualty,
such porcelain frailty,
my own selfish Morality,
life's ebbs and flows,
so red was the rose,
bleeding like my terminally ill soul,
a man apart,
lost without his unborn,
unseeing heart.

Remember you told me, "You'd be the death of me,"
the price of our love was too high,
such a sad and lonely goodbye,
alone inside my empty soul,
I cry,
I cry.

*Freshly uncapped, poured into a tall glass and served
chilled in the wine bar of my mind …*

Licking

Into the fire,
into the flames,
I commit your body to eternal damnation,
oh, what a thrill,
oh, what a release,
as I watch the flames flicker,
licking at your cast aside shell,
you shall never be at peace.

Damage,
the wrecking ball of my life,
savage, ripping,
tearing at my feelings, my flesh,
heart in my mouth,
your mouth,
life drastically headed south.
Into the fire,
into the flame,
burn,
fucker burn.

Freshly unpacked from the steamer trunk of my mind ...

Go with Grace

Her name whispered on the mists of angels' breath
and in the muted songs of tortured banshees,

Death and her Disciples follow her like an addict to the
needle, like an ice-cold scalpel to a pulsating hot vein.

The beauty in her snow kissed vanity,
the pain in her pay per view insanity,
dripping tongues like melted popsicles in hells sizzling
sun,

The beauty in her uncaged reality,
whispers and moans,
her soul is out on permanent loan,
there's something arousing in her deadly unearthly
sexuality.

Blood dripping,
reaper tipping,
unrelenting soul removal machine,
running high on 100 octane gasoline,

Snow White goddess possessed by an unkept promise,
left at the alter but never again,
now she's mankind's revengeful beautiful pain,
she's no man's leftovers, no man's door mat.

Her bloody vitriol drips
as the chrome blade rips
and leaves an eternal stain.

*Freshly brewed and poured piping hot and served with
steamed frothy milk in the coffee house of my mind ...*

A Tear in Your Reflection

A naked bulb, just hanging,
flickered, highlighting the polar loneliness
of my whiter than non-yellow snow, coloured bathroom,
I looked at my reflection
in the unforgiving, all-knowing, and all-seeing mirror,
I wish I could change the profile picture.
Sadly not.

My mind flickered,
a long-forgotten memory, stuttering into view,
so long I'd kept it buried,
but not deep enough it seems.

I felt the warmth of her smile,
the lightness of her touch,
I swear I could smell her perfume.
Then a new warmth,
trickling down my cheek,
I looked closer in the mirror,
the reflection showed a projection,
I could see her in a teardrop,
faint but there,
like an old oil painting,
a hidden detail unearthed,
then like a forgotten 80s band.

The teardrop explodes,
still the reflection is there,
I splash some cold water on my face,
and look for a clean shirt to wear.

Freshly dusted off, topped up with alcohol, and ready to sing Happy New Year. In the year 2023 of my mind ...

Before

Before there was ash,
there once was a flame.
Before there was a river,
there had to be rain.
But the bigger the river,
then the bigger the flood.
The deeper the wound,
the redder the blood.
The bigger the mountain,
the steeper the climb.
The riper the grape,
 the sweeter the wine.

With great power,
comes greater responsibility ...
To show your real self,
Takes real honesty.
The less one knows ...
The less you've read.

*Freshly pulled from the dusty memory banks of my
Sinclair ZX 81 mind …*

Bleed for You

Time, so much taken for granted, so little left,
I go to the water's edge, I open myself up to you,
my life's essence flowing out, mixing with the icy cold
river, mingling like an artist's pallet of aqua's marines and
blues,
slowly overrun by the deep redness of my pain …

I walk slowly into the water.
The cold takes my breath away for a moment ...
now I only feel numb ...
is it my time, time, time.

Wait a second ... what am I doing,
when my time is up the reaper will surely come for me,
why am I making his job easy,
this is not my time to die,

I lay there, bathing in the glory of living,
clutching my wound like a newborn,
the reality of my mortality,
is suddenly my priority.

Time, time heals all wounds, this is the real hope,
I am hope, you are hope, if we believe then we are all
hope,
we just need to give ourselves time, breathing space ...
time to …
heal, time to think.

*Freshly dug up, staked, and reburied in the vampire's
graveyard of my mind …*

Ode to Buffy

Her warm blood trickled down my face,
drinking in her essence, bittersweet,
just like the day,
Oh Buffy, it didn't need to end this way.

I look down into the dark emptiness of her eyes, lost,
but still clinging on to her soul,
like a forlorn ship in the eye of a storm,
trying not to capsize.

I cradle her lifeless frame against me,
I feel her heart finally exhale,
her warmth escapes me,
so sad it had to be you,
I wish you had been able to stay
Oh Buffy, it's a shame it had to end this way.

The eternal battle of conscience,
the double edge sword,
of being a vampire, a writer, a poet,
and Buffy the vampire slayer, fighter.

But, even in death,
her fading presence still tries to take away my last
breath,
Oh Buffy.

Freshly inhaling the beauty and natural drama
that surrounds us …

On the Wings of the Wind

Beautifully chaotic,
swirling, almost hypnotic,
her name carried on the lips of the four winds,
whispers and moans,
the way an old wooden house groans
under the weight of anticipation,
bracing itself against the western winds' blustery
infatuation.

Oh, she is such a tease,
sends me into a tailspin with effortless ease,
she's the eye of the storm.
A perfect storm,
when our seven worlds collide,
her dreams and feelings are locked deep inside,
but underneath that armoured but ethereal skin,
there is such an angel forever watchful
    within.

Freshly taken from the Hits radio station coffee table book,
The St Clair Poles ...

Solitude in the Sand

Memories of past times,
landscapes somewhat blurred but I remember them ...

Like the ancient remains of a long-lost shipwreck
or the prehistoric ribs of a great sea beastie.
But no, they were the Groynes.

Solitude stands in the shifting sands,
majestically controlled by the unwavering hands
of father time.

I remember them
like a half-eaten row of Cadbury flakes,
set against the far-reaching sky,
wrapped in its grey mohair overcoat,
scented with an air of metallic forlorn,
dripping lavender hues into the turning,
churning tides.

This beach,
littered with good intentions,
like the Groynes
a relic of the past
or an example of simplicity in its invention.

*Freshly massaged in, right to the scalp, then rinsed out in
the home hair salon of my mind ...*

The Desolation of Love

Too beautiful to live, jealousy is such a potent emotion,
too perfect, to be taken seriously,
fear of what you don't understand,
that superhuman notion.

Skin deep vanity,
scantily clad insanity,
fuck it, let's 3D print nature,
everything can be improved,
natural only dies,
fake plastic flowers last forever, and ever and ...

The misappropriation of conscience,
the Desolation of love,
the complete absence of faith
in what lies above.

Beauty is more than skin deep,
beauty is everywhere,
not to suffocate or even replicate,
but it is there to appreciate,
jealousy of a creator,
penis envy of the ultimate animator.

Beauty in its reality,
natural in its variety,
Different is what different does to not be the same.
Like humanity is its own calamity.

Freshly picked up from the multitude of fallen white rose petals, crying down from the heavens above ...

The Reality of Tomorrow

Dave Grohl sang "it's times like these you learn to live again,
it's times like these you learn to love again" ...

No truer words have ever been said
But it is times like these you find out
That family does not have to be blood,
family are the ones that show they care
in whatever big or small way....

Depression and grief often go together
but they can be separated,
they are not symbiotic,
at times maybe chaotic
and sometimes seemingly unending.
But with the lightness of the new day dawning,
we can find a new perspective,
we can still be reflective and even protective ...

It's times like these we learn to live again.
Hold the memories close,
keep your heart open,
laugh out loud,
cry with the angels,
and dance in their tears,
conquer the unknown ...
laugh in the face of your fears ...

*Freshly unearthed and dusted off from the dark attic
of my mind ...*

Ungiven

Borrowed, but not stolen
Unearthed, but not exhumed
Taken, but not by force
Uneasy, but not necessary
Alone, but not by myself

Messages written in the sand,
thought balloons penned by hand,
a heart surviving,
but not living
the love ungiven,
to the heart untrue
A worthy adversary,
call it blasphemy
the love of a lifetime,
said the caller to lifeline Missing,
presumed taken,
without a sound,
under the cover of darkness,
ungiven was my authority,
my innocence was taken,
by the secret minority.

Freshly picked from the low hanging branches, and gently placed in the infinity basket of thoughts in my all too busy mind …

Waterline

I saw her down by the waterline,
Skin glistened like liquid bronze in the warm sunshine,
eyes a bluish hue like blueberry wine,
a vision so clear,
sadly, frozen in time
but I saw her there.

I saw her down by the waterline,
I don't recall the day,
I don't remember the time,
but I will never forget her lying motionless
by the high tide line,
I saw her there.

I saw her down by the waterline,
Lifeless, emotionless,
this wasn't her time,
a life cut short by the silent voice
in her sad and dark mind,
her only way out was the peace and tranquility
of the waterline …

Sadly, I saw her there.

*Freshly planted in rows close to labour day, for new
potatoes on Christmas day in the raised garden
of my mind ...*

The War in My Head

Nobody wins, the war in my head,
Everyone loses, this war in my head.

The battle lines have been drawn for what seems like
    forever
both sides struggling, fighting in fixed bayonet entrenched
    warfare,
one day the side of sanity charges forward, unleashed
    positivity,
awash with hope and unity for the future,
drives the dark army of negative thought underground,
if only they would stay down in their darkened tear
    streaked, bruised, and blood blistered bunker.
Where they belong.

But like any great adversary, they don't,
they lie in wait, starved of light, love and hope,
they fester, whispering deathly sour but sweet nothings,
the army of dark thoughts has no grace,
they hide behind a singular smiling face,
a mask you see but don't really see or really know.

There is peace at the moment.
But let us not be complacent, let us not forget
how quickly the turning tides of sanity can change,
be vigilant against the dark army of negative thought,
they cannot get a foot hold,
or I could be lost forever,
buried under a stack of heavy darkened Jenga thoughts
    and emotions,
pinned down in the trenches of lost dreams and despair
    ...

Least we forget nor cease to remember ...

Freshly unpacked from the weekly grocery shop in the pantry of my mind ...

Proof of Life

Breath in, breath out,
through consciousness and thoughtless doubt,
Like a vein pulsating in a scarecrows neck,
don't stop and check,
for proof of life, or a trace of death ...

From here to eternity,
remember the golden rule of taxidermy,
test for death,
just in case there's proof of life at the tip of your scalpel,
at the pointy cutty end of your Smeg designer knife.

But if you do,
try and check for a pulse in that old scarecrow's neck,
be mindful.
He was never alive in the first place,
maybe recheck the tin man
and that bedraggled lion, too.
They said they were alive,
but I thinks they were a lying ...
and that wicked witch of the west
well, she dissolved in the tears of
the unmade dying.

*Freshly dredged up from the bottom of the ocean by the
super yellow submarine digger of my mind …*

Shiny Things

To the bottom of the fathomless sea,
under the shadow of a watery grave,
feathering its nest,
stowed away like an unwelcome guest,
a gleam in its little red eye,
enough to make a one-legged pirate cry ...

You must be off your driftwood rocker,
if you want to look through Davey Jones locker,
the key to the siren's song,
what lies beneath ...
"Why is a raven like a writing desk?"
said the creator of fantastical beliefs.

Cry me a river,
or an ocean of salty tears,
while I struggle for a single breath,
inhaling in this sea of emptiness.

While all the time it sits there watching, waiting,
a ruby glint in its eye,
then it silently slips into its concealed cosplay costume
of a long dead magpie.

Freshly untied, undone, and set free, in the zoo of collectable soft toys of my mind …

Tears Flow

Bad, bad things happen.
Sad, sad things happen.
Tears flow, when sad things happen ...
Blood flows, when bad things happen ...

Sad but true,
my tears mix with the blood drips,
like an artist's pallet of eternal sadness.

Sin deep,
the angels weep,
the reaper mops the blood-streaked floors,
he might take life but he can't abide mess,
he always says, "a clean scythe is a happy sharp scythe."

Angels and demons,
the good, the bad and the dead.
Writing quietens the voices
begging to be heard in my head.

*Freshly washed, spun, and hung out to dry from the
laundry hamper of my mind ...*

The Metaphoric Doors of Life

Metaphorically speaking,
for the longest time in a short uneventful life,
one laden with sadness, darkness, and strife,
a stut, stut, stuttering heart,
missing a beat every time they're apart.

Love in a time of loneliness, smallness, and heavy
heartedness.

Thoughts float like lead balloons
from the small-minded parishioners,
counting their blessings
as they count their dirty money.

A simple man with an empty heart,
a small mind filled with unanswered questions
that will stay a mystery forever,
if only their fear of failing
hadn't kept them from being together.

Freshly unearthed from the rubbish heap out the back,
cleaned off, and polished up, in the eBay auction site
of my mind …

Waiting for the Rain

Can you feel the heat in the air ...
I can see it shimmering mysteriously.

The dogs search for anywhere cooler,
under the kitchen table on the cold floor,
that's a favourite place
where they try and melt into the vinyl.

The deck is no place for bare feet or even sensitive
paws,
sadly, dogs and cats don't do jandals
but I do,
essential footwear for this time of year.

At night the garden calls to me like a siren song,
encouraging me to get the watering can
and shower the parched plant life in cool, life-giving
wetness,   but wait, there's a smell on the breeze,
undefinable but I know it anywhere,
it's on its way,
glorious lifesaving Rain,
small petite droplets
growing in size and magnitude,
it's a downpour,
drink it in.

The wait was worth it,
embrace the watery moistness.

*Freshly cut out and stuck in the dog-eared brag book
of my mind ...*

Ode to the Night

Welcome, oh sweet sanctity that is the darkness of the
night,
Let the soft flow of the moon
guide us to our chamber of dreams and peaceful
slumber,
Let us then be awakened,
refreshed by Ra's golden fingers
as they gently caress our nakedness
into the warmth of a new day dawning,
Until we meet again,
oh, sweet sanctity of the night.

*Freshly dug up, shaken off, washed, and boiled with salt
and served with lashings of butter in the allotment
of my mind ...*

Demons Inside

She was his,
he was hers,
but then his own personal demons got in the way ...

The chaos and angst inside his head,
a clockwork heart bleeds for the unmade dead,

Fighting for life,
fighting for a single breath,
crossing over the painful threshold,
inhaling in his emptiness

The eternal battle of heart versus ego,
in a past life and in the afterlife,
trick with a knife,
quick as you like,
death is just a feeling,
trick with a knife,
ends your beautiful life,
love is more than a feeling

Demon's inside,
there's nowhere to hide,
mind like a steel box,
a trick with a knife can't even pry open its rusted old lock,

Tick tock goes the eternal clock,
tick tock, tick .... tock, tick .... tock .... forever.

*Freshly scrawled out on bits of my own skin from the
madness of my own mind ...*

Last Writes

He blew his mind out in a haze,
smoking gun,
a worn-out pen,
the last words still in his gaze.

The contents of his mind
spilled out onto the pieces of paper strewn about,
across his drunken and disorderly desk.

His head resting in his clammy hands.
Empty, spent, but ... satisfied, job done,
The absolute joy or dreaded curse
the knife edge of being a writer, poet, and freedom
fighter.

Freshly dug up and moved to a more secure location
from the shallow grave of my mind ...

Housekeeping Tips #7

An unidentified person asked,
"I have a large red stain on my white shag pile carpet,
anyone have any ideas on how to get this out?
Could be red wine; could be blood.
Asking for a friend." regards Vito.

Well Vito, in my experience
the best way to get rid of a pesky red wine/blood stain
on a lovely white shag pile carpet
is slightly on the extreme side but necessary, so ...

Health and safety first, gloves and eye protection,
(don't want to make the situation worse),
leave the broken bottle/body in situ,
start from the wall and roll tightly into a large tube shape,
fold in the ends and tie up
with some old pantyhose, duct tape, or ripped up clothes.
Make sure any loose glass, wine corks, or wallets,
identification cards, etcetera are contained inside.
Carry out to a waiting car/blacked out van,
and dispose of at the most available building site,
laying fresh concrete foundations.

Sit back, relax, and embrace
those gorgeous freshly polished hardwood floors.
Oh, and remember
to wipe down those walls, cupboards, and doors.

*Freshly penned by my own hand on the writing desk
of my mind ...*

Head Case

A head full of emptiness,
a bottomless pit,
of darkness and despair.

Forced thoughts,
don't try so hard,
if it's meant to be,
it will be,
so, for now just let it be.

An empty thought chamber full of nothings,
the hoarder of my lies,
the stuff that dreams are made of,
but barren as a cloudless sky.

Like a recently plundered shallow grave,
the words stumble out,
oxygen starved,
depraved.

I look in the mirror,
searching for my lost smile,
finding it,
keeping it,
growing it,
now that might take a while.

*Freshly thrown on the turntable and molded into a clay
sculpture in the art studio of my mind …*

Sin Deep

The itch that I can't scratch
the words that I can't say
the sins of my past,
the thoughts that won't ever go away.

The life that I once lived,
in some rose-coloured rear view,
the love that I once gave to a heart untrue,
still, I thought that I was so strong
that the truth would force me through.

I'm only now understanding
what it meant to have known you.

Freshly picked from the crab-apple tree of my mind ...

Unique

Unique in their motivation
a masterpiece in their own creation,
gifted with the superpower of imagination
never lower your expectations,
life's a journey not a stay-cation,
but treasure the memories along the way,
remember this sisterhood,
remember this day.

People come and people go,
but the friendship seeds grown at Tolcarne
will forever grow.

Be strong, be brave,
love yourself and seize the day,
as you go, some tears will flow,
and we'll miss you more than you'll ever know.

Stay unique, stay boutique,
never stop learning, never stop searching ...
for life's answers that you seek.

*For all the schoolgirls, past, present, and future at Tolcarne
Boarding Residence*

Freshly unrolled and laid out on the dining room floor
of my mind ...

Thoughtless

A careless whisper,
maybe an off-the-cuff comment,
followed by that full length legs,
crotch and finally face look.

Thoughtless,
unspoken,
unintended,
but not invited.
Deliberate but unplanned,
learned but not through upbringing.
Self-taught arrogance,
barely camouflaging our own ignorance.

Thoughtless, so do we care less,
or just think less,
humility,
humanity like peas in a pod they are not.

A careless whisper,
that ill-fitting glass slipper,
not a Cinderella moment ...

*Freshly unearthed from the dank bubbling, bottomless pit
that is my mind ...*

Shall I

Shall I compare you to a lonesome mirror
starving for an ounce of attention,
while seeking some vanity encrusted,
mercury dipped,
looking glass redemption.

Shall I caress you as if you were a prickly thistle,
with my sun-bleached touch,
pain in every movement,
still I need you so much ...

Shall I love you for your flowers of Scotland,
flourishing with purple,
while echoing your resilience, fortitude and bravery ...

Shall I treat you like a masterpiece, as life imitates art.
Committed to the earth, where once you came,
to then with time be renewed with abundant life again.

With thanks to William Shakespeare ...

Freshly harvested from the negative thought fields
of my
mind …

Split

Madness, silent and seductive, calm but obsequious,
a tightness in my mainframe,
 just above my main brain,
guilt descends, time transcends
the room disappears into the night,
so come and take my hand
and lead me from this place of sorrow.

Bad, bad things happen,
sad, sad things happen.
When sad things happen, tears flow,
when bad things happen, blood flows.
My tears mix with the blood drips,
like an artist's pallet of eternal sadness.

Through the haze,
straining to see through my red streaked and crazed
eyes,
I faintly hear my mind's own mantra,
echoing on the wind.
Make good choices,
don't listen to the voices,
If only I'd listened …

Freshly taken prisoner by the thought police in the Christmas cake scented table decoration of my mind ...

The Reaper Goes Festive

On the 13th day of Christmas, the dark lord gave to me.

A RED EYED SCYTHE SWIPING,
SOUL STEALING, UNFEELING,
REAPER IN A SANTA CLAUS SKIN SUIT.

The only present I'm getting this year
by the looks of it is my death notice in the local paper ...
Merry FUCKING Christmas ya filthy animals ...

*Freshly taken out and polished up to go on display in the
trophy cabinet of my mind …*

Nip and Tuck

Our tight rope act of human frailty,
a messy combination of self-loathing and thoughtless
vanity

The eternal search for our external youth,
the serum of love
that's 10% proof, 5% reality and 85% "what the f@#k!"

Behind the masks we all at times wear,
is the realness of life,
laced with sadness,
dressed with honesty so rare.

Like the plastic surgeon
that's scared of a needle prick,
we're scared of the label "natural,"
in case the name sticks.

Freshly separated, then thrown in the front loader,
washed, rung out, spun out and hung out to dry on the
summer's morning clothesline of my mind ...

How Do We Disappear

A song by one of my favourite singer songwriters Lana del Rey was
the inspiration for writing this....

These days in all its technological, stealthy ways,
just disappearing isn't as easy as it perhaps once was.

Some days when you're just so tired of the world
and its soul-destroying ways,
you just want to walk into the washed-out skyline
of a long-forgotten watercolour painting and just
disappear,
just fade away,
painlessly but not
needlessly,
thoughtfully but maybe a little selfishly.

Where do we go now,
when we want to just disappear
where is our vanishing point ...
maybe it could be simpler and closer than we thought
I just disappear inside my head,
see my thoughts,
uncover things that are better left unsaid,
fall into the words I try to write,
ideas blinking like stars in my mind's starry, starry night.
Disappearance is different to irrelevance.
My preference is just to disappear ...
but with poise and just a little elegance.

Freshly trimmed and manicured in the nail salon
of my mind ...

A Dog Called Misery

For some time now
I've had a little dark coloured dog shadowing me.
I think I'll call him "Misery."

As I walk through this world,
he softly patters a little ways behind,
reminiscent of the dark fog
that sometimes clouds my mind.

When things are going well,
he is nowhere to be found,
but these days I can't seem to catch a break,
so, he's always around.

They say misery loves company,
and that is plain to see,
the darkness in my mind
is the despair you never see.

*Freshly rebooted from the national lampoons vacation
of my mind ...*

Appealing to Our Conscience

The cost of human kindness,
for just a dollar a day,
the price we pay for our blindness,
will hide the troubles away.

Our faith is tested, our conscience arrested
while the downtrodden keep dying,
their babies keep crying,
and while the war lords get richer,
the world misses the big picture.

The price on our humanity
is only matched by the cost on our sanity,
maybe it's merely our own Vanity.

Freshly traced from the outline of the mountainous
dreams of my mind ...

Lizario

Like a fallen, golden snowflake,
riding the air currents like a shining sky surfer.
The merging of the fairy nymph world
and the mysterious reptilian Corinthians.

Lizario, golden impresario, winged fork tongued avenger,
cherub smile, bullet with butterfly wings,
like when Lana del Rey sings ...

The gift of fight or flight,
such an elegant sight,
Medusa's touch,
flittering,
glittering,
with the gift of second sight.

That singular sparkle,
flickering
in the darkness
of the darkest night

Freshly heard in whispers on the cool breath
of the western wind ...

None of Us Has to be Here

It's true ... none of us has to be here,
I heard this on a television program ...
at times some of us don't want to be here ...

sometimes there is a battle being fought in our minds,
in our souls, in our lives ...

Whether to give in to the negative thoughts, traumatic events,
and slings and arrows that life can throw at us
and go quietly into the darkness of the eternal night,

Or stop, breathe in, exhale, take time,
look into ourselves, look with eyes wide open.
Find the good, the friendships, the love, and the things
no matter how miniscule
or seemingly unimportant they might be,
that make keeping up the fight,
holding on 'til the new dawn,
and realizing just how much
we actually have in our lives,
how much there is to live for.
Worthwhile.

Don't give up without giving yourself time to realize
there is something, some reason to keep up the fight,
none of us has to be here ...
but it's good you are here.
Don't give up on yourself.

Freshly opened with a rusty can opener, poured into an awaiting pot, and served piping hot on hot buttered toast in the dusty kitchenette of my mind …

Snips and Snails and Black Painted Nails

Good girls go to heaven,
bad girls have all the fun,
up to my bollocks in fishnets
and not an orange roughy in sight,
they could be quite fetching ...
if they weren't so fucking tight.

Nails as black as my dark and bottomless soul,
deep like the darkest night,
shining like onyx stars
hidden in plain unclothed sight.

Snips and snails, a handful of blackened nails,
I followed a trail of broken dreams to your door ...

For Robyn.

*Freshly taken down gently from the pop starred poster
walls of my mind …*

Visions of Me, Versions of You

In the distance,
channeling your existence,
strike the pose,
synthetically grown nose,
searching for your soul in your eyes,
while trying to find the truth in your lies.

Visions of me,
the face I was born with,
the only one I use.

Versions of you ...
How you feel today effects what filter
your inner self decides to choose ...
Every time you use it,
a little more of the genuine you is what we lose.

Visions of me, Versions of you ...

*Freshly unearthed from the musty cobwebbed spooky
cellar of my mind ...*

The Redemption Tree

The change of life tree,
hang your hat on it or hang yourself off it.
The choice is yours.

For those who know,
you can never run away from the problems
of the past or the present,
but sometimes the future is harder to deal with than the
past,
at least that's behind you,
redemption,
or maybe accepting,
in life there are some things you just can't change,
one thing you can change
is yourself.

But it ain't easy,
the events that made us,
can also break us,
and in some cases forsake us,
those nagging, biting, hope sapping thoughts.
You're not good enough, intelligent enough, or ...
worthwhile enough, for love, for yourself.

Soul Reaper, Self-belief Stealer, Sin Dealer, Fate Sealer.

I hung a noose off the redemption tree,
that past cracked rear view mirror life is what I see,
Que sera, sera, whatever will be,
will be or not, at the sound of the beeeeeeep,
repeat or
Delete.

Freshly trimmed, plucked, polished, and manicured in the beauty salon of my mind ...

The Departed

Smooth cold awaiting stainless steel
Warm quietly clotting blood
The recently Departed,
unbreathing and undone.

Supine in position awaiting deaths physician

Looking heavenward with eyes wide shut,
taking in or playing back,
what must it be like as death becomes us all,
hmm, he wonders
as he makes his incision at the point
of the sterno clavicular articulation
and prays for his salvation.

Freshly scrubbed on a time rounded rock, rinsed off in the river, and hung out to dry on the willow branch of my mind …

Puddles

Wandering aimlessly down this old gravel road,
lost in my mind,
out of step,
and out of time,
searching for something,
the one thing,
that will kick start my heart,
make my soul sing,
the meaning of life,
make sense of the strife.

The tsunami of uncorked thoughts,
awash in my main brain,
just above my mainframe.

All of a sudden,
my thoughts seem to turn into to a trickle rather than a
flood, wandering steps turn into a minefield,
carefully stepping around and over thought puddles
in case they are deadly manholes of deceitful thinking,
if I stand in one,
will I lose myself forever
in my thoughts.

Freshly dug up, washed off, and boiled with a little salt in the cosy kitchen of my mind ...

Shallow

As shallow as it's skin deep,
but as hurtful as a thoughtless comment from a faceless creep.

Sticks and stones,
broken homes,
the blood still bleeds red
from the unmade dead.

Scratching the across the surface,
you know just where the hurt is,
twist of the knife,
a small sacrifice,
paybacks a bitch,
ain't nothing but a stitch ...
intime, but it's healing
these razor cut deep scars of mine.

*Freshly dredged up from the salty, silty seabed
of my mind ...*

The Decision Tree

To be or not to be,
should I stay or should I go,
do we see what we want to see,
or do we only hear what we want others to know.

Decisions laid bare,
still blissfully unaware,
my nerves, tighter than a torture dangle's harp string,
the pain that only being human, can bring.

Which way is up,
how far down to the ground,
still can't believe I climbed up this far,
so near, but oh so very far,
oh, how wonderful it is to be,
held by the lofty arms of the Decision Tree.

I carved our initials in the Decision tree,
for richer or poorer, you said to me.

Right there I made the decision,
to be all that you can be,
live long and prosper,
see all that you can see,
you are important, but ...
what you see
isn't always what you want it to be.

Sad but true.

Freshly uncapped and poured into a large glass in the shady beer garden of my mind ...

The Other Side

So, what if I told you death was survivable,
how could I show you?
With proof undeniable.

Shall I crucify myself,
Bleed 'til I'm so pale,
then YouTube my resurrection,
now that would be some tale.

Death is only the beginning,
the end isn't always nigh,
the key is believing in something,
not just to justify.

It is true life is for living,
as we see on this whole worldwide,
but that doesn't mean when my time comes
I won't see you on the other side.

Freshly dredged up from the silty depths of my mind ...

Turn a Deaf Ear

He said what happened
to turn it into such disrepair
life, life happened,
so much to say, so little heard.

A deaf ear,
finely tuned by an Italian Vespa mechanic
to only hear words that were never spoken,
none were uttered from those chattering mouths
wired shut for fear of sinking
from those loose lips silently thinking.

Like ships passing in the night,
getting stuck in the Suez Canal,
thoughtless jibes and heartless words
that drip off satanized tongues.

A tender loving ear
will eventually turn tone deaf
if never hears
the beauty of sweet nothings.

Freshly tapped out on the android keyboard
of my non apple mind ...

The Redemption

As someone famous once sung ...
mistakes, I've made a few ...

Unbreathing, undone, a life unlived,
my nerves like a classical guitar ... highly strung,
facedown in a pool of false beliefs,
my soul in pieces,
my heart in my mouth,
but still lying through my teeth.

As I walk along this lonely beach
on the road to my redemption,
I pick up the leftovers of my past,
the offcuts and broken promises,
this lonely beach is littered
with lost dreams and good intentions,
on the road to my redemption.

*Freshly picked from the low hanging branches in the
abundant orchard of my mind ...*

'Til the End of ...

Eternity, a place, a time, somewhere we may find,

I'm gonna love you 'til the end of time, sang Lana del
Rey,
even if there's no reason,
even if there's no rhyme.

Even if it takes a million years
and my heart is rained upon by a billion angels tears,
I will love you 'til the end of time.

Love you 'til the end of the line,
commit the seven deadly sins,
be crucified for all my crimes.

I will still love you 'til the end of time ...
take it to the end of the line,
knowing you will always be mine.

I will love you 'til the end of time ...

Freshly printed out with hand carved potato stamps in the kindergarten classroom of my mind …

Scented

Friday autumn sky,
wrapped in its grey mohair overcoat,
scented with an air of metallic forlorn
dripping in lavender.

*Freshly unbuttoned, eased off my shoulders, and thrown
in the laundry hamper, in the upstairs bedroom
of my mind …*

Stealing Time

This life,
to some a marathon,
to others a sprint,
to everyone ... a journey ...
but to where, to what, and when?

There's no after pay in the afterlife,
the finality hurts
like the twisting of a plastic surgeon's knife.

Stealing Time,
second by second,
hour by hour,
'til the end of the line,
or 'til our line of credit runs out,
living on borrowed time,
nothing is ever for free,
one day they will come to collect.

Simon says do this,
the reaper says I never forget a face,
no matter how much work you've had done,
no matter how much time you tried to steal,
there ain't no thing as deal or no deal.

Love and kisses, Death

Keeping it real since forever.

*Freshly dug from the flats of the Himalayas, dried, and
put into shakers in the Himalayan pink saltshaker
of my mind ...*

My Own Personal Soul

Carefully chosen at the time of conception,
Stretched to size,
immaculately inserted,
but without recollection.

Some are slow to grow into theirs,
a soul to please,
a soul to squeeze,
and some will die before they ever know.

Soul saver,
dream maker,
I was soulless and so I cared less,
then on the road to my recovery,
I made a startling discovery,
when my heart's in need,
then it's my soul to bleed.

Plant the seeds and they will follow,
fulfil the need,
secure a tomorrow.

*Freshly collected, licked, and stuck in the slightly rare
stamp collection in the back of my mind ...*

One Small Step for Man

Dangling from invisible threads,
the shining moon drags us from the shadows of
darkness, lighting the way for the deeds of a few,
the dreams of some and the hopes of many.

Its shimmering presence is somehow reassuring
in an alienated, unwavering way.

We go to sleep with it,
make plans under it,
and even play golf on it,
and yet this glimmering shiner of a thing hangs in there,
in its powerful,
unearthly shining way,
like the big cheesy thing that it is.

*Freshly unfolded and unfurled then hoisted up the
memorial flagpole of my mind …*

Find Me

Somewhere out there,
beyond the testosterone splattered chain-smoking
skyline,
amongst the broken shards of the once revered amber
glass,
you may find me,
or maybe part of me,
the part I used to be,
what's left of me isn't what it's cracked up to be ...

But if you come looking,
don't do it halfhearted,
you can't turn back once the journey has started.
Is it a rescue or is it a recovery,
be warned,
I might not be that amazing discovery
you were hoping for,
but to be honest,
I really don't care,
if you look,
if you search,
if you cry out my name
you may find me there.
Find me.

Freshly plucked from the neighbour's peach tree and made into a delicious dessert in the country kitchen of my mind …

Devil's Child

Once upon a time,
in a far-off place,
the devil made a play,
for the whole damn human race.

In his greedy plans,
between his toothy smile,
in his bloody hands,
he held nothing but a child,
and looking in its eyes
he thought he could see for miles.

What was happening to him,
being loving just wasn't his style,
nothing but a child,
the war with God
paused for a while.

When the mists had lifted,
he realized what he had been gifted,
in his hellish hands,
was the future of his fire and brimstone land.

*Freshly taken from the laundry hamper, popped in the
machine, washed, and hung on the washing line
of my mind …*

Apart

Torn apart,
the rose red confetti pieces
of my mortally wounded heart.

If I,
could wash it all away,
turn back the hands of time,
or is there another way?

If I,
could take the pain away,
would that help sooth my love,
so, you might live another day?

Could I,
wish this manic life away,
start over,
reset our love,
would you finally stay?

Could they,
look forward to a day
when differences don't rule the world?
Yea, that would be the way.

*Freshly rung out, dried out, and all cried out in the
solemn heart-shaped tear collection box of my mind ...*

Heart-shaped Tear Collection Box

I cried a tear,
you wiped it away for me.
I held you near
and I felt your heart beat for me.

In my mind I see you smiling,
forever young and free.
In my heart is where
you will always be.

I save the tears I've cried
in a special heart-shaped collection box,
to keep them safe from the horrors
of time and forgotten memories.

Tears,
the essence of my soul that my sleeve wears ...

Tear-streaked cheeks,
rung out like an old dish cloth
but nothing lasts forever,
that's why I collect my tears in the heart-shaped box,
to remember that even when there's happy good times,
around the corner things can change,
remember, so we don't forget ...

*Freshly marinated, slow cooked then pulled and served
in the bao buns of my mind …*

Internal Bleeding

Her hurtful barbs pierced my vulnerable heart,
a seemingly unprovoked attack,
the injuries were extensive,
massive internal bleeding,
my poor injured heart,
hemorrhaging love.

Fond memories and sweet dreams
like a knife to a ripe tomato,
the wounds could be fatal,
fatal if left unloved,
uncared for, and untouched.

Internally bleeding,
a love transfusion my heart was needing,
a gentle brush of her lips
or maybe a shoulder just to cling to,
my heart skips a beat,
normal service restored,
lost frozen
love finally thawed.

Freshly taken from the vegetable compartment of the
refrigerator and thinly sliced in the spring kitchen
of my mind …
(Based on a true story.)

Mosaic

An unfinished art installation,
a big mosaic of my life,
so many tiles,
some still in one piece,
but so much fragmentation,
pieces of me,
pieces of you,
some of that,
a bit of them,
and a smidgen of when,
but, I'm struggling with a couple of blank spaces.
I've labelled them for future reference.
The biggest space, is, WHY?

I marked it with a tear drop.
I think it will remain forever empty
and will always make me cry.
The other space is marked REGRET.
The tiles for that space probably aren't all broken yet.

A life in pieces but not in ruins,
a threadbare tapestry,
that is my own personal artistry.

*Freshly pulled from a deep hole to sit around and drink
tea, in the Mad Hatter's tea party of my mind …*

Oh, Alice

As strong as she was,
as clever as she thought she was,
she never knew how good she was.

The power of one's heart,
the strength of one's resolve,
can overcome even the largest obstacle, if …
only you have faith in oneself.

Oh, Alice, did you really need to grow that tall.
Growing up eventually comes to us all...

Through the depths of my imagination,
sifted through the Mad Hatter's ego,
wreaking of desperation,
the song remains the same,
off with her head, off with her head,
paint the roses, paint the roses red.

With thanks to Larkin Poe for their inspiration.

Fresh and fruity from the fruit salad can of my mind ...

Paper Thin

Hearts like books,
Read and used time and time again,
Pages, layers, well thumbed, dog eared, marked with
pain.

Patience, like pages,
getting thin with age,
delicate to the touch,
only saved by the gentle book binder
or soul mate that cares just as much.

My heart beats slow, like the book
I pick up then put down, then ...
pick up again with renewed anticipation,
heart beats faster, a well written masterpiece,
our love at peace.

The End.

Freshly unwrapped, put on to plates, and served with lashings of tomato sauce, in the fish and chip dinner of my mind ...

Feeding Time

There's blood in the water and ice in my heart.
Grey skies rain down the bitterest of tears.
The blood streaked forever moving skyline,
teaming with insatiable life,
waiting, circling.
Suddenly a trick with a knife,
another lost life.
The ocean churns,
a broken heart yearns
for the newly departed
and come aparted.

Yesterday's heroes
now tomorrow's fish food,
the birds keep a circling,
the reaper is a lurking.

A calmness follows a killing frenzy.
Somewhere in the distance
a radio
plays ...
Birds flying high,
you know how it feels ...

*Freshly shuffled then cut and dealt evenly, in the Caesars
Palace of my mind …*

Sleight of Hand

Time is ticking,
out of control,
head down,
joker played and aces high

The magnificent green of the table
is swallowed whole by the darkness
of the dealer's eyes,
perspiration in spades,
good fortune though
is running on empty,
no matter how hard you try,
the house always wins
in the end.

The devils in the detail,
heads down,
sleight of hand,
and your fate is in the unshakable hands of a higher
power,

win with the utmost grace,
but lose with style,
lose with honour,
a game of lost chances,
you win they lose,
it's up to you
which path you decide to choose.

*Freshly picked from the entwined sprawling grape vine
of my mind ...*

To Be Wanted

We crave,
from the cradle to the first innocent kiss,
the first taste of real love to ultimately our final earthly
grave …
to be wanted, to be loved, to be … touched,
physically, emotionally. even mentally.

We crave,
to see her gorgeous smile,
with fingertip feather light softness
trace the lines of that beautiful face ...

We crave,
to hear her voice, her laughter,
that could bring a room to life,
like setting fire to the night, blazing bright,
filling the night sky, flickering with devilish glee ...

I crave,
the salt from your tears,
as I hold you, your whole-body
quivering with the pain and tiredness after all the happy
years ...

I crave you,
but now all I can do is visit with you,
I remember still, I will never forget,
so much to be thankful for,
our life together,
but the loneliness is intolerable,
I crave you always,
even as you rest in your well-tended grave …

Freshly stripped of my Street skin and thrust into a
waiting pair of hungry speedos, in the beach hut
of my mind …

The Bach

The sign said
"Relax, Unwind, Enjoy"
Who could argue with that …

I slipped out of my 9 to 5 mortality
and put on something lighter,
something more comfortable,

I sat down in one of the easy chairs,
poured my emotions out into a tall glass,
added a squeeze of self-loathing,
some ice and stirred,
downed in one gulp,
now time to feel the sand between my toes,
the salt spray on my lips.

Sitting here, the air is so quiet,
tranquil and free except
for the rhythmic waving of the hands of the sea,
and the gentle cries of the gulls that fly by,
so peaceful, so graceful,
and soaringly high,

The Bach,
a first aid kit for the soul,
take it off, hang it on the line
and let the sea winds recharge, soothe, and re-energize
it,
now put it back on,
your personal superman suit,
ready to take on life again.

*Freshly placed into terracotta pots with heapings of
potting mix then sprinkled with baby unicorn seeds and
watered with my own tears ...
in the magical garden shed of my mind ...*

A Town called Shameville

The town built on humanity,
with foundation stones made of our own arse kissed
vanity.

Where the sun never rises,
in the grey industrial skyline,
Shame, shame by any other name is still shame
Shoulders stooped, a turned down smile,
The residents of Shameville
where self-forgiveness went out of style.

Under the cover of darkness,
without my recollection or authority,
my innocence was taken by the ruling minority.

We have all done things
we all have a past,
we all deserve a second chance,
even if it's our last.

Shame is the silent killer of our time,
shame bleeds depression,
oozes self- loathing and breeds' hate.

Shameville.
a small mid-western styled town
with an ever-changing population,
some folk will rise up
and shed their thin veneers of shame,
like a snake shedding its now useless skin ...

Some will sadly succumb to the sinful ugly stain,
that can cover our lives
like an inky black disturbing stain
on our spotless, sanitized family name,
then there's the ones,
condemned to walk the lonely streets
and unwelcoming avenues of
Shameville ...
Like faceless forlorn shadows of their once proud selves.

Shameville
Population, infinitely forever changing.

Freshly unearthed and dusted off, from the dark and gloomy attic of my mind ...

The Gift of Imperfection

The gift that keeps on giving,
that amazing gift of imperfection,
running hand and hand with natural selection,

some gifts aren't given ...
borrowed, but not stolen,
unearthed, but not exhumed,
taken, but not by force,
uneasy, but not necessary,
alone, but not by myself.

Messages written in the sand ...
thought balloons penned by hand,
a heart surviving but not living,
a love ungiven to a heart untrue.

A worthy adversary, in a Greek tragedy,
the love of a lifetime
said the caller to lifeline,
missing,
presumed taken without a sound,
under the cover of darkness,
ungiven was my authority,
my innocence was taken,
by the silent minority.

Freshly mixed, and deposited into tins to bake in the Thermowave oven of my mine …

The Past

Past, present, future,
three relatively ordinary words
but all linked
like three different organs in the human body,
all with their own separate functions
that ultimately work together to keep it from dying.

The Past,
sometimes depending on the situations,
can almost be bipolar,
one day it can be as smooth as a stainless-steel egg,
then suddenly it can turn jagged,
like a broken razor blade,
slicing through our present,
upsetting our nicely planned life,
like a fox running rampant in a hen house,
and putting our future in peril.

Can we ever escape it?
Do we just keep on running from it,
or do we turn and try and face it,
as hard as it is,
as hurtful as it might be,
sadly, no matter what,
the past never goes away,
leave it behind,
where it belongs.

Fresh, but hastily written in the sand SOS, on the castaway island of my mind ...

The Willow Tree

Underneath the weeping willow tree,
I kissed my love,
underneath that tree.

Yes, I kissed my love underneath that tree,
I stole that kiss when I was three,
she was four but as cute as could be
I kissed my love,
underneath that tree.

Underneath that tree
when I was three,
nothing else mattered in the world to me,
that kiss underneath
the Weeping Willow tree,
my life would never be the same you see.

A life beyond that Weeping Willow tree,
the life when I'm older than when I was three.

Our names still scratched on that old willow tree
Yes, I kissed my love underneath that tree.

*Freshly pulled from the hanger, dusted off and tried on
for size in the walk-in wardrobe of my mind …*

Silence, the Quiet Killer

Depression,
lately a media obsession,
but …

Depression
doesn't necessarily kill,
Silence kills,
Holding it in kills,
Being staunch kills,
losing the will to live, kills.

Depression
doesn't have to be fatal,
it is survivable,
Talking,
Trusting,
Believing in yourself,

It's undeniable,
we are all perfectly imperfect,
But …
we are all,
Worth It.

Freshly taken from the memory vaults, of my time as an embalmer, many, many moons ago in the normally locked memory chest of my mind ...

Someone's Daughter

Even in death she was beautiful ...
she was pale ...
but that wasn't anything new,
her skin was like fine China
but with an inner fragility,
now she lies there with a porcelain coldness
to match her finely sculptured features.

Even in death she was no fading flower ...
how can someone hold the floor
without being able to say a word ...
her mere presence a gift
maybe a hidden superpower.

Even in death she was alive
in her family and friends 'memories.

Sometimes there are those who are taken too soon,
we don't know why,
maybe they are needed elsewhere,
in another world,
in another time.

Even in death she was beautiful.

Freshly dug up from the veggie patch of my mind ...

A Tear in Our Reality

I'm so tired,
no one wants them anymore,
how long I don't know,
since I started selling my tears
to put a down payment on a second-hand soul,

Ebay, Amazon and Trade Me are my nemesis,
no one wants to buy from an unregistered tear trader,
no matter how cheap and pure they might be,
it's all synthetics these days,
chemically generated,
factory propagated,
and artificially flavoured
with fake Himalayan pink salt.

The "one size fits all" claim
doesn't always fit these days,
they don't make souls like they used to,
mine has a hole in it,
no amount of duct tape can fix it,
sadly each day,
more light is let out and more darkness seeps in.
cry me a river,
said the retailer of tears.

Freshly unhinged from the chest of bat shit craziness in my mind's attic ...

Gifts from Above

The world is out of focus,
trouble and madness seems to be magnified,
like looking through a rain drop
in the eye of a hurricane
in my own watery eye.

Out of focus, wrong resolution,
I spy in my minds little eye
something beginning with WET,
these gorgeous raindrops,
these globules of moistness, life giving,
thirst quenching, drought preventing,
but then sometimes unrelenting flood inducing,
death producing crop reducing ...

Water, the gift of life from above,
we drink in its wateriness,
then bathe in its slithering glory,
we dance and sing in it,
rejoice in it, even drown in it.
It's a bit of a balancing act,
this water is too deep,
this water is too dry,
this water is just right,
said the little blonde-haired girl
with a fixation for breaking into
decent law-abiding bears houses.

Gifts from above,
highly underrated
especially when you're saturated ...

*Freshly dehusked, cracked open, and poured into an
awaiting glass in the pina colada bar of my mind ...*

Imperfect Masterpiece

Like a dark purple crushed velvet dawn,
smeared across this October skyline,
bittersweet, incomplete, life tragically edited and left,
like the unwanted scenes cut and left unfamous,
unknown,
on the cutting room floor.

Rewind, no, fast forward,
nah actually just push delete,
those dreams they had in life,
those scenes destroyed with a needle, with a knife
a bitter, poisonous pill to swallow,
washed down with the rose-coloured tears of those
crying,
drowning in their rivers of never lived tomorrows.

Unborn hearts never to feel the pain of first love,
unseeing eyes destined only ever to look down from
above.
Those unfulfilled dreams,
never to be filmed scenes,
like the writer that's just run out of ideas,
out of time, out of ink, left to just think.

A life's unfinished manuscript
drowned like an unwanted gift in the bathroom sink.

Life is for living,
sadly, for some it will be also for the taking,
our future,
our fate is mostly of our own making.
Make an imperfect masterpiece,
be the artist.

Freshly fed, watered, and put to bed, in the dog motel of my mind …

Orange is the New Black (Jumpsuit)

How do they go back to normality ...
when locked doors and plastic forks are their reality.

A rest home for the criminally disenfranchised,
where their hopes disappear before their eyes,

Incarceration,
desperation,
deprivation,
just some words of alliteration
compared to choosing a new flag for the nation.

Life behind bars,
with no visible scars ...
just don't scratch the surface
cause that's where the hurt is.

Freshly washed, conditioned, teased then blow dried, in the hair salon of my mind …

Famously

The time before,
before they …
before they wanted more,

My mind wanders aimlessly,
through the depths of my depression,
over the mountains of my life's obsession,
soaring high above past loves and lies but ...
with no recollection.

I wish I had known myself at a deeper level;

Without the clandestine sarcasm,
without the pressure to "play the game",
the joker behind the mask,
trying to ease my inner pain,
always trying,
inside ... crying,
but like a moth to a flame,
always trying,
to please,
flitting around,
but still sadly not yet seeing the light,
living but dying a little,
simultaneously,
but not famously.

Freshly measured into an awaiting filter, steeped to its
fullest, and poured into an eagerly accepting cup
of my mind ...

That Apple ...

Once upon a time,
in a far-off land,
a man and a woman
met at the fruit and vegetable stand,
and that's where it all began ...

The sweetness of our sin,
sour to our taste,
but not sour enough to stop ...

Our world,
our modern-day Roman holiday,
we are up to our elbows in it,
sin deep,
what is the need for procreation?
Can't be because the world is low on population.

Swipe right, or left,
swiper no swiping, said Dora the underage explorer,
the internet, the highway to hell,
through the wild west styled last frontier of our deviant
minds,
a hell on earth, so what's it worth ...
how much for your pound of flesh,
asked the black-market second-hand soul trader,
also specializing in discarded tears
from the unborn dying,
the done trying ...

We follow trends like an addict to the needle,
like a hamster on an oversized wheel,
running, running,
fueled on Red Bull,
running to stand still,
the faster we go
the bigger the mess,
and time isn't ours to steal,
are we there yet, are we there yet ...
no ... not yet,
but...
We're on our way,
from happiness to misery
oh yeah ...

Freshly collected and chopped into thin pieces, ready to set fire to the night, in the wood pile of my mind ...

The Tragedy of the Mirror

Deep as her last forlorn look,
black as the pebbles at the bottom of a babbling brook.

The tragedy of the mirror,
my reflection doesn't show the ugliness of my soul,

The tragedy of its reflective honesty,
only highlights the fault in my selective humanity.

The tragedy in our porcelain vanity
crumbling like my fragile sanity.

For the 51, the lost souls of Christchurch …

Freshly poured into a large bowl, covered in cold milk and a little cream, noisily eaten in the cereal for dessert night of my mind ...

Shattered

Heaven is calling,
angels are falling
Love lies bleeding
at Hell's bloody door
Dreams are scattered,
trust is shattered,
Like shards of glass
on a stormy seashore.

Head in hands,
digging through sands,
piece by piece
our innocence evermore,
Is a notion,
the incoming ocean
will wash our hearts
clean from Hell's bloody door.

Can a heart be awoken,
after being so broken?
Can our trust be repaired
after being so smeared,
with the blood of lost love
and dreams never more?

Freshly popped into the awaiting dulce gusto machine, to make smooth strong coffee in the bench coffee maker of my mind ...

Steal the Light

I just found a book on Amazon ...
Steal the light.
Forever the lonely and
longest night.

The night holds many mysteries,
fears and ancient histories,
the darkness,
my ode to the night,
the guidebook on how to steal the power from the sun,
oh, the sweet sanctity of the night,
darkness, oh sweet darkness,
kissed by angels' wings,
dream delicately,
dream deeply,
block out the sun,
that's why I wear my sunglasses at night.

Steal the light,
blackout the night,
thank God for the gifts of second sight,
hello my old friend
From the dark warmth of my mother's loving womb
to the earthy dark depths of my forever tomb,
death,
the eternal elephant in the room,

Stole the light,
turn on the night
Forever.

*Freshly taken from the frozen foods section of my mind
and placed in a warm water bath of my heart ...*

The Murdering Witch

Blood,
nature's spirit level,
spill it on the ground,
if it ain't flat it'll run ...

Shallow,
just like it sounds,
bury them lightly,
expect them bodies to float with the tides,
with a flood,
bury them deep,
the blood will seep,
into the ground,

Bury them deeply,
a precaution to take,
least you want their souls to escape,

Death,
bury them deeply,
or sinisterly and discreetly,
they will haunt you from the ends of the earth,
'til the end of time.

How much blood do you have on your hands,
you filthy witch,
you murdering bitch,
the dead will rise,
before your dark eyes,
your time has come,
thy will be done.
Bury her in a standing position
there won't be no heavenly transition,
shallow not deep,
her pain with death won't cease,
this murdering wench
will never rest in peace.

*Freshly peeled, thinly sliced, and laid in an oven proof
dish in the potato gratin smelling kitchen of my mind ...*

The Sister Hood

The space between us,
the air around us,
the common bonds that bind us,
and when times get hard and life seems tough,
if we think we have nothing at all,

We still have Us.

*Fresh washed, dried, and polished to a mirror finish in the
car grooming garage of my mind ...*

The Drowning Man

Gulping for a single breath,
Inhaling the emptiness,
Trying to fend off the incoming hopelessness,
Then suddenly   calm,
a stillness,
descends upon him,
A realization the fight is done,
The end is nigh,
A single tear greets the sea
in a salty forlorn
and lonely goodbye.

Freshly taken out, polished within an inch of its silvery self, to then be put back in the top drawer of the sideboard of my mind ...

My Voice

Can you hear me? Is anyone out there ...

It feels like I'm inside an old black and white television,
tapping on the glass screen and trying to get somebody,
anybody's attention.

Silently screaming inside my head,
the sound is deafening,
my voice,
if it is my voice,
echoes against nothing,
it sadly falls on millions of deaf ears.

Unchained melodies
of melancholy harmonies
played on paper thin instruments
made from the veneer
of a long dead petrified satinwood tree.

Strung by a caffeine infused silkworm,
too blind to see the complete futility of his life's work,
like a middle-aged man who feels the need to twerk.

Enjoy the silence.

*Freshly washed, hung out, then ironed and put into the
undie draw of my mind …*

Magical

An image in my mind,
a kind of perfection in its place,
a memory of a time,
that may fill a future space.

A fragrance on the wind,
her name only ever heard in whispers,
dripping off the tongues of angels,
like delicate clouds of ginger kisses,
the dream of her touch,
a vision just to cling too,
so magical in so much
as it's only in my dreams,
that it could ever come true.

Magical, fantastical,
surreal, and ethereal,
whether it's a dream or real life,
the answer's immaterial.

Freshly taken from the refrigerator, beaten flat, floured, egg dipped, and crumbed to be then fried to a golden brown in the chicken parmigiana dish of my mind …

Alone

Loneliness,
is one example of an activity
you can do by yourself   alone,
no one else.

Alone
For some a superpower,
to others a curse,
like being locked in a velvet upholstered cage,
strung out in a haze,
like being lost in the centre of a maze,
God, doesn't he move in mysterious ways …

Alone,
some of my best conversations have been by myself
although they can be a little one sided ...

Alone,
can anyone imagine having no one really believe you,
to then be flailed, nailed, and crucified ... alone.
Up on that bloody cross,
for all Humanity
but just you,
for others to stop and stare,
watch you slowly, lonely and painfully
DIE …
alone.

Alone,
can be many things to many people,
Alone in a prison cell at Christmas,
Alone in a houseful of family
where everybody's talking but no one's listening,
Alone on a deserted island
with only a volleyball to talk to ...

Alone in my head,
some thoughts are best left
                              unread.

Freshly picked from the low hanging branches of the branberry pear tree …

Grief

SADNESS
ANGER
SADNESS
FUCKING ANGER
HELPLESSNESS
TIREDNESS
EXTREME SADNESS
RESENTFULNESS

SADNESS

FORGIVENESS.

*Freshly scrubbed on a large, rounded rock then rinsed off
in an ice-cold stream ... in the "off the grid" camping spot
of my mind ...*

Auto Reject

I'm the kinda guy that likes the personal touch,
I don't do auto detection
or algorithms that delete selection,

Automatic for the people,
problematic and autocratic,
not terribly diplomatic.

I write what I feel
and I feel what I write,
so there might be the odd,
fuck, shit or worse
that flows out of my pen
when I write late at night.

Fast forward, rewind, play, and eject,
that's the only machine
I know that's designed to reject,
(my 80s mixed tapes).

Fresh, but sleepily poured into an awaiting mug and
gulped down in the late night coffee craving of my mind
...

Black on Black

The darkness of the darkest night
the unwanted gift or curse of second sight,

Black on black,
that long forlorn journey back,
from the depths of my black-washed empty soul,
the pitiful remains of my tattered and torn heart,
showing the scars
of where the slings and arrows of heartache
have taken their toll.

Black on black,
the unending night,
the loss of willpower and need,
no, the want,
to give up the fight.

Black on black,
the stark whiteness of that far away light,
like that unreachable star
that voice,
like a siren song,
don't listen, don't look,
don't go towards the light.

Our end of days in our own pointless way,
we give up the fight.

White on white,
the hope and the promise of Dawn's first light,
reborn, alive, rejoice.

*Freshly ripped off, unboxed, and flung across the lounge
in the early Christmas morning gift opening of my mind ...*

Silent Repose

Her camouflaged expression,
a puzzling mixture of tranquility and deep thought ...

Her face,
marked with time,
like a road map to the stars ...

Statuesque,
and in a state of undress,
still secretly elegant in her unabashed ebonized
nakedness.

Alone she will be,
like the very last truffula tree.
but we should not be so judgmental,
it's not a crime to just be ornamental
just kinda sad in a way.

*Freshly grated, then generously sprinkled over the
steaming roast vegies, in the Jamie Oliver kitchen
of my mind …*

Spiralism

Loss,
at a depth too deep to comprehend,
rock bottom,
a life in pieces,
the dreams that descend,
then land in a crumpled pile,
faith at an end.

Still a sliver of light sneaks down,
bringing a ray of hope,
transcending a darkness unending.

The climb,
out of obscurity,
from the teeth marks of desperation,
on the spiral staircase steps of elevation.

Ascending,
the double helix of life,
reaching the summit,
cool rain on my face,
the sun in my eyes,
Spiralism,
a dream,
a dream of idealism,
now a realism.

Freshly eaten with cheese and Huntley & Palmers cream
crackers, (reduced fat ones of course), Danish salami,
and a little relish in the late afternoon snack time
of my mind …

The Left Behind

Traipsing through each day from dawn till dusk,
the degree of loss is undefinable,
grief and its lingering memories infiltrates itself
into every facet of everyday life,
an object,
a song,
or a conversation.

Oh, how I long for the sanctity of the night,
when you return to me in my dreams,
beautiful,
free from the sickness and pain
that so consumed you.

I miss you,
and I crave for the darkness of the night,
to see you again,
until then my love,
until then.

*Freshly heated to over 1000 degrees and poured into
moulds in the bell foundry of my mind …*

Dirty

Like the final curtain coming down on a Broadway
musical,
the dirty greed-streaked industrial skyline
closes in on the lightness of another
God given day.

Dirty like my porn hub mind,
empty as a scared to death corpses bladder,
and heartless,
as an entitled arse who doesn't give a fuck.

Human beings / Being human,
same words, but poles apart,
like a modern-day Napoleon Bonaparte
and the height restriction
on a fairground attraction,
can't get no satisfaction,
no, no, no.

S.O S. messages written in the sand,
save our fucking useless, mean-spirited souls,
the earth is in rebellion,
like a caged for far too long wild stallion,
ready to take the power back.

Humanity's headstone reads,

　　　"The useless Fucks, they knew too much."

Too soon.

*Freshly washed, stuffed, trussed, and put into an oven at
180 degrees, mmm roast chicken, in the cozy kitchen
of my mind …*

Life, Death, and Everything In-between

They say we are born,
we live and then we die.
but there must be more,
I saw my mother,
talked to her,
held her hand then.
She wasn't there,
she had gone,
her earthly body may have been left,
but it was like a well-used shell,
I know my mother was not there,
but where she was
I'm not sure.

Life and Death
and the bit in-between,
that in-between bit can be short,
or it can be long,
I have seen a lot of death in my life,
in my previous profession,
an embalmer in a funeral home
(True story by the way),
but it hasn't done anything
to help explain where we go
when we have completed that long or short bit
in between being born and dying.

The romantic answer I guess
is if we have led a decent life,
we go to heaven,
but where is that?
It's always been portrayed as up
But there's only sky,
clouds and
Space,
the final frontier.

Or we get to,
if we have been Bad,
go down into the depths of Hell,
until it freezes over at least,
and with climate change.
Hmm, might not be that long.

I do believe we go somewhere,
I have seen something leave,
out of the corner of my eye,
like a light flicker,
a ripple in time,
our hearts cry as their soul's fly,
somewhere only they know where,
but I know they are somewhere …
yeah, they are there.

*Freshly removed from its sanitized, tamper proof
packaging and popped into the toilet bowl of my mind ...*

My Only Vice

Between a rock and a not so comfy place,
caught between a laugh and a tear,
could be both yet ...

Have you ever got to that stage,
That stage, the age,
of self-doubt,
of reasoning the unreasonable,
of thinking the unthinkable,
of finding suddenly your taste has changed,
and life seems ...
undrinkable.

Is it just a stage
the middle age,
maybe we just need to listen to Bob Seager
and "turn the page."

I think sometimes we think too much,
we dig too deep,
get too fixated on when to sow
and when to reap.

As most of us have realized,
it doesn't matter how hard we try,
we don't control time,
we don't control the weather,
the earth doesn't listen to our lies,
the earth knows we aren't that clever.

The more we try and own this universal stage,
mother earth just sighs and turns another page.

Here's the thing,
how many pages do we have left,
before it just says …

THE END

Freshly cut and put through the shredder in the allotment
of my mind …

Postage Paid

Love letters written by hand,
notes left in haste,
hearts and arrows traced
in the disappearing sand.

An imaginary card,
I dreamed I sent to you,
with an invisible message written
but no one knew.

Postage paid,
love unmade,
words unspoken,
hearts still broken.

The embers still smoulder,
in my dreams
I still see you,
But my heart seems
much colder.

Love letters written by hand,
so loving and so tender,
sadly, all come back marked,
"Return to Sender."

*Freshly inspired by Nirvana's Heart shaped box from the
stereophonic attic of my mind ...*

Pain Less

One of the things in life
I find most difficult
is seeing friends, family, people you care about,
in pain or suffering,
for whatever reason
and feeling completely helpless.
Kurt Cobain said it best,
"I wish I could eat your Cancer when you turn Black" ...

Death Eater,
pain reliever,
life retriever,
wouldn't it be awesome to have those superpowers ...

But the reality is we don't,
sadly, it sometimes seems like God is playing.
Well God ... with our lives,
deciding on who lives,
who dies,
and who lives in terrible
debilitating pain in their life.

I really wish ...
"everybody hurts ... sometimes",
wasn't true,
but sadly it is ...

For Bonnie.
Credit to R.E.M and Nirvana ...

*Freshly dug up and transplanted into the raised garden
bed of my mind …*

Endless

A journey to the ends of the earth,
steep like a towering mountain side,
like a diver descending the depths of the ocean deep.

A love,
a never-ending passion,
deep as a chasm,
endless as an unfinished book,
stark and unforgettable as a last cracked rear-view look,
the last great crusade,
such a waterfall of emotions,
a sad and forlorn macabre parade,
but of course, it's all in God's name,
not for the money,
not for the fame.

Killing in the name of
Oh what an immortal tale,
for God, for king,
and of course,
the endless search for the Holy Grail.

Freshly scraped and shoveled off the grass and deposited in a biodegradable bag in the dog poop collection of my mind ...

Pieces of Jesus

In pieces I fall,
exposed at your feet,
In pieces maybe
but not in defeat,
Arms wide open,
palms out turned,
A crown of bloody thorns
and sun-bleached burned.

Unbreathing,
undone,
another nail and the damage is done,
Is he the king of the Jews,
or just the salt of the earth?
Or the Devil in robes
standing on hallowed turf.

We follow like an addict to the needle,
like a scalpel to a vein,
The joker behind the mask
trying to ease his inner pain.

A handful of nails,
a crown of bloody thorns,
a game of lost chances
and Jesus with horns

*Freshly opened with the old can opener from the top
draw of my mind …*

Stab in the Dark

The power of voodoo, who do? you do .

The pain behind my eyes,
hides a deeper, darker pain,
an immovable stain,
on my soul ...

Like a thousand tiny ice picks,
tearing a deeper hole.
Dental floss thread and golden needles,
some wounds are too torn to ever fix.

Who casts the spell,
who makes the decision,
where's going to be,
the next painful incision.

Sins of our past,
like a bed of nails,
you made it,
now you have to lie in it ...

Snips and snails,
a handful of nails,
tattooed and torn,
a crown of bloody thorns,

The pain you do,
is your own voodoo ...

Thank you to David Bowie and a certain film, Labyrinth, for the opening.

*Freshly packed in a small carry-on bag, and stowed in
the luggage locker of my mind ...*

The Gift of Flight

It's a freezing cold Dunedin early morning,
Shelley has just dropped me off,
5.15am check in,
said our goodbyes
and I boarded the seemingly tiny
wind-up propeller airplane,
dang, a real one would have been nice.

It's an odd feeling, sitting here,
squeezed in like a sardine next to another
sardine that I have never swam with.
Watching the guy outside spray de-icing fluid over the
airplane.

It's an odd feeling, this gift of flight,
45 minutes and I will be touching down in Christchurch,
this amazing gift of flight,
and just look at that out my window ...

Oh, what a beautiful sight,
pretty cool, this gift of flight.
time to disembark,
and onward to Dare to lead.
too early to say
but I know I won't be turning gay for Brene.
My arse has gone to sleep,
roll on Thursday and I can do it all
again but homeward bound this time ...

Freshly shaken out and pegged on the washing line
of my mind ...

Soul Cleaning

I woke up today,
looked in the mirror,
my reflection didn't show,
only the ugliness of my soul.

I emptied my laundry basket into the machine,
amongst the sulking undies and slithering mismatched
socks,
I could see my dirty thoughts,
unfulfilled dreams, and unmade love,
all tied up in the shitty off the cuff comments of everyday
life.

I'm hoping on a hot wash,
the stains on my soul suit will come undone,
if not, it might be time for the emperor's new clothes,
indecent exposure here I come.

*Freshly driven at high speed over hastily laid road spikes
in the police chase of my mind ...*

Family Ties

She said she wanted to visit family,
an overgrown cemetery
in a grey windswept shell of a town,
littered with the amber remnants
of the pride of the south.

Her brother dead at 22,
car wreck,
successfully ground himself into the tar seal,

Dad, heart attack at 50,
Jimmy's pie still on his breath,

She looks at me with sadness and hunger in her eyes,
says I could really murder a burger and fries.

Freshly picked from the garden and placed in a Moorcroft
vase in the front room of my mind …

Blood Lies

Microscopic,
strangely chaotic,
particles of deceit,
infiltrating,
humiliating,
then suddenly hibernating,
once their nihilistic damage is done.

White Blood cells,
red blood,
we need both types of cells so who the hell cares,
what colour our selfishness wears.

Robotic,
symbiotic,
yet uncommonly philanthropic,
we go through the motions
savouring the emotions
'til we get our fill,
does anyone know the meaning of lying straight in bed?

Is it a notion,
the incoming ocean,
will wash away the blood lies
that have held siege in my head.

This bloody love starved beach
is littered with good intentions.

Fresh in my mind, though so long ago …

Deep Thought

Buried deep, like a lost artifact,
like a forgotten memory,
secretly hidden away,
but actually, in plain sight.

Extracted by a master
in the dark arts of thought extraction,
using an ancient hand-tooled
over exaggeration contraption.

Self-taught,
the science of deep thought,
lost in one's self,
lost in the haze,
trapped in the maze,
the Bermuda triangle of my mind,
skimpily clad thoughts
pass each other like ghostly ships in the night
only to be swallowed
by the ethereal nothingness of my mind.

So deep …
endless,
bottomless,
the pit of deep emptiness,
so deep …

Freshly taken as gospel, but possibly mistaken in what I
overheard ... in the crowded hospital cafeteria of my mind

...

All Things to Everyone

My mind ...
like a used-up tea bag,
it's dangling string,
tight like a tortured fallen angels guitar string
but silent in its beaten down opinion
as only a lifetime of lovelessness can bring.

My thoughts ...
like the millions of tiny stars in the darkest of night skies,
blinking yes,
maybe or yeah nah,
but drowned out by the night ravens cries.

My heart ...
stretched and pulled this way and that,
feelings tight like my tracksuit drawstring,
until Snap!!

Pain and solitude
like only a broken heart can bring.

All things to everyone,
and nothing to some,
there's no in-between,
and nowhere to run,
somewhere,
across the universe the night withdraws.
Here comes the sun ...

Freshly folded and pressed in the Chinese laundry
of my mind …

Dream Flower

Dream flower,
it is you who have the power
dream flower,
up there in your ivory tower
dream flower,
getting blinder by the hour
dream flower,
the opposite of sweet is sour.

Sunflower,
climbing, fuelled by solar power,
a moment in history,
now is the hour
dream flower,
strung out in a haze
dream flower,
baby I'm amazed
dream flower,
locked in a violet crumble cage dream flower,
the whole world's a stage.

Sunflower,
climbing, fueled by solar power
a moment in history,
in the darkest of hours.
dream flower,
underneath it's just a mess
dream flower,
perhaps it's all just one big test
dream flower,
of course,
it's what I do best
dream flower,
 love yourself,
forget the rest.

Dream Flower?
Deadly Nightshade,
hmm well played.

Freshly unfolded, hung on the flagpole but out of respect
... at half-mast ...

The Last Wave

At peace at last, no more are we under her protection,
surrounded by her treasured handbag collection.

A lifetime of service, honoured now in this time of
sadness,
her bright sense of fashion matched her smile
so filled with gladness.

Mother of our Commonwealth, her children and our
nation, through war and peace,
her wave now will cease,
she's at peace ...

The Queen is dead
long live the king,
such strange words,
the likes my ears have never heard ...

She lost her prince,
he was always by her side but two steps behind,
a heart broken,
never to be mended,
still her public face so filled with grace,
but alone.
together now in eternity,
Queen Elizabeth,
you stood the test,
you did your best,
now at rest,

I now sadly wave goodbye to you.

Freshly taken too soon from the awaiting collection of wonderful human beings that leave this world before their time in the sad, sad tear-streaked grief compartment of my mind ...

Fallen Stars

They allow us into their lives bit by bit,
through technology we seem to almost know them
but we don't,
we never really will,
but that doesn't mean we don't feel the pain of their
passing
as if we really did
know them,
I guess it's part of our complicated human frailty.

But I know myself
I have cried at the loss of someone I don't know ... really,
Elvis, Jeff Buckley, Chester Bennington, Chris Cornell,
Taylor Hawkins, Jeff Beck, to name a few ...
now Lisa Marie Presley ...

Death is such a final thing,
their music and presence made our hearts sing,
they fulfilled their need so our tortured hearts could
bleed.

God bless them all.

*Freshly unwrapped, bitten, and dunked into my hot coffee
in the morning tearoom of my mind ...*

Adventure Time

The journey began at Dawn's deftly touch,
caressing the mountain tops,
gently warming,
thawing,
I could not have wished for as much.

I set out, striding forth,
hopes of success gathering in glassy beads
before they slithered and trickled down my neck.

To prove to myself,
that the earth was not flat
and the moon wasn't made out of wensleydale cheese,
that was my quest,

these make-believe adventures,
some might say are frivolous daydreams
and a waste of productive time,
these dreams,
these farfetched ideas,
while I lie here,
confined inside this paralyzed unmoving body
in this starched white sheeted prison of a bed,
these pipe dreams of fanciful adventures,
the only thing that keeps me from completely dying,
alone in my head.

Freshly nailed, strung up, and hoisted up, in the
Crucifixion Fields of my mind ...

Chaos Theory

We're doomed, doomed I tell ya ...
stability calls for a steady hand on the wheel,
global warming,
that big grey climate change elephant in the room ...

Meh, no big deal.

Is there an order in our disorganized disorder.
Chaos theory,
fuckery at every turn,
when will ...,
will we ever learn the big ole hamster wheel turns,
the oil burns,
and God does it make my stomach churn,
my kids, your kids their kids,

A beautiful human being gone too soon once sang,
"is this the world we created"
sadly yes it fucken is,
 "the world we devastated",
right to the bone ...
We made it on our own,
we did it to ourselves ...

On our end of the world Headstone, it reads:

"Here lies Humanity, the stupid fucks ...
they knew too much. too soon."

Freshly taken by polaroid camera in not so good lighting in the sultry and dusty 1970s photo studio of my mind ...

All Things Must ...

We are born, thrust naked, crying and afraid,
into a world we don't recognize or know,
like a human jigsaw puzzle
and we are just another piece looking for somewhere to
fit in.

Oh to fit in, the right fit, not a tight fit, might chaff a tad,
but just be glad you're not the odd one out,
the high school dropout,
the one destined to please everyone but themselves ...

George Harrison sang "all things must pass,"
not a truer thing has been said,
grief too will get easier,
with the passing of time,
but things will sneak up and hit you where it hurts,
with no rhyme, with no reason.
enough to knock you off your feet,
leave you unable to move,
like your tied to your very own railroad track,
oh Zac, Zac, Zac, Zac,
if only you knew ...
I whispered to you
How much you were truly loved,
Sad ... but true ...

In memory of our lost soul who couldn't find his way home -
Zac Marston-Senior

Fresh and alive after a brief loss of writing MOJO ...

Dreamers of the Past

How many tear drops
does it take to cause a flood,
how many broken hearts can we suffer
'til we finally run out of blood.

Hearts with bones,
living lives without meaning,
giving our love,
without feeling.

Where has our innocence gone,
what happened to the writers
of all those lost love songs.

where have all the flowers gone,
the dream weavers
and the daydream believers,
maybe they were all only alive in their songs ...

*Freshly stolen from a used car salesman, driven like I
stole it, and abandoned like a shed skin in the dusty
desert planes of my mind ...*

Dirty Blade

Breakfast in the house of the never again rising sun,

His dirty blade,
I use to spread the house made chunky marmalade,
on my whole wheat toast,
my bread flame licked from the ludicrously hot fires of
hell,
toasted to perfection,
my calendar marks time,
it's almost Christ's resurrection,

Gosh,
where has the year gone,
just seems like yesterday,
in the midst of my mind's infirmity
I crossed the line to a dark eternity,

His dirty blade,
the reaper Slade,
the eternal price you paid.
Homemade is always better than house made
marmalade ...
just saying ...

Freshly nailed, screwed, and bolted to the back fence in the DIY shed of my mind ...

Dark Lands

The deepest, darkest back roads,
snaking, slithering
through the twisted thought forests
of my unrelenting sleep preventing head.

A reality scarier
than what is advertised as the truth,
who knew ...
but my truth just might be different to yours.

Dark lands, stark and uncompromising,
like a backhander that doesn't leave a mark,
like the cold-blooded slaughter that never leaves a stain.
in God's name,
hark can you hear the angels sing,
glory, glory, hallelujah
the devils in the detail,
he sees right through ya.

Do you see his eyes,
looking out from the trees,
the air goes cold,
space and time fold like galactic origami,
breath.
Breath in,
exhale,
now RUN towards the light,
before he hammer's the final nail.

Freshly buried in an already forgotten corner of the
overgrown allotment that is my mind ...

Dark is the ...

Blue was the sky high above me,
brown is the grass,
parched and sunburnt,
with no relenting in sight,
One big mess of super deep-fried hotness.

Dark is the night,
still is the air around me,
clammy is my skin,
the sweat beads down my chin,
another sleepless,
restless night begins ...

I crave ...
the smell of incoming,
life-giving,
thirst-quenching rain ...
taste it on my lips,
dripping off my fingertips,
cooling the internal,
infernal fire,
burning deep within my main brain.

John Hiatt sang, "and it feels like rain"
Lord, it feels like rain,
splashing down on the windowpane,
oh let there be rain.

Freshly boiled, rinsed, and drizzled with olive oil and chopped parsley, in the Italian-styled kitchen of my mind …

Between a Laugh and a Tear

How big is the distance,
what causes the resistance,
between a laugh and a tear,
as the years go by ...
Sometimes we laugh
Sometimes we cry,
but that space between us,
the air around us,
the love within us,
some things grow,
some things lessen,
so what is between a laugh and a tear.
that is the question.

The truth is, not much.

As the world turns,
the spark of love burns,
cry together,
laugh together.
Yell, scream, cry at each other,
laugh hysterically at each other,
Cry ... uncontrollably,
unconsolably,
at the loss of the other, cry,
think of the memories,
cry, laugh,
remember ...
remember the in-betweens.
Between a laugh and a tear,
the distance is how long or short you make it.

*Freshly trimmed, dusted, and watered in the indoor plant
sanctuary of my mind ...*

Death is More Than a Feeling

Come quietly, be gentle, I said to the night,
Seething, writhing, it's under my skin,
Lying, conniving, the countdown begins.
Sinister intent, hopeful that my soul will relent,

The voices say, "don't let them in, don't let them win"
yeah, yeah, yeah, "don't let them in, don't let them win"
yeah, yeah, yeah.

Cut off its head, check under your bed,
Death is more than a feeling,
seeing behind those blue greenish eyes,
then I will start believing,

Your will is your own,
whispers and moans,
the seeds of hope have been sown.

The voices say, "don't let them in, don't let them win",
yeah, yeah, yeah, "don't let them in, don't let them win"
yeah, yeah, yeah.

Bury it deep,
the flesh won't keep,
cut out its eyes,
smother its cries,
stop the monster from seeing,
death is more than a feeling,
yeah, yeah, yeah.

About the Author

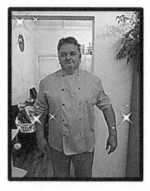 Ross Leishman actually wrote his first poem for an English project at high school when he was 16. It was called "sitting on a beach" and now 53, he still remembers it word for word, sadly that's where his writing creativity stopped or ... Paused. Fast forward to 2009, he had recently separated from his wife and their children and was living alone. Misery loves company and so he started writing again. It was a great way of getting those pesky dark demons out of his head and onto paper where they belong.

As he got older and greyer, he became more comfortable and confident, sharing his soul with whoever wanted to see it. His life had been full of ups and downs, but he found the most inspiration in the darker, tragic things, events in life, and those dark melancholy thoughts. He writes about what he sees, what he feels, and what he hears.

A couple of years ago, he started doing this little introduction before each poem; "freshly deposited into tins and baked at 180 degrees in the bread bakers' oven of my mind", and it became his trademark.

He lives in Dunedin, at the bottom of the South Island of New Zealand, with his wife Shelley, their two dogs, a cat, and a turtle. They have three children: Darceah, Bryn, and Bonnie. He is the Head Chef and Food Service Manager at Tolcarne Boarding School where they cater for and look after 155 boarding school girls.

He has a liking for Italian scooters and motorcycling. He loves music and his influencers would be Jeff Buckley, Rodney Crowell, John Hiatt, Lana Del Rey, and Tom Petty.

Recently, he was privileged to be included in the Open Skies Poetry Anthology Volume 1 and Dark Reflections, Southern Arizona Press' The Poppy: A Symbol of Remembrance and Ghostly Ghouls and Haunted Happenings and Raven's Quoth Press' Evermore Volume 2. He has also been fortunate to have one of his poems published in a photo book, The St. Clair Poles.